Applesauce

by **Dana Meachen Rau**

Reading Consultant: Nanci R. Vargus, Ed.D.

Marshall Cavendish
Benchmark
New York

Picture Words

apple

apples

applesauce

core

pot

seeds

spoon

tree

grow on a

.

Pick to make for you and me!

Take out the . . . .

Take out the .

Get another .

We need a lot more!

Put and sugar

in a .

Be careful now.

The gets hot.

smells good.

We will have it soon.

Eat your 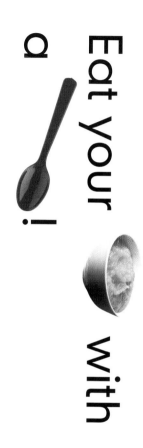 with a spoon!

Words to Know

careful (KER-fuhl)
to be safe

grow (groh)
to get bigger or older

Find Out More

Books

Murphy, Patricia J. *A Visit to the Apple Orchard*. Mankato, Minnesota: Capstone Press, 2004.

Thoennes Keller, Kristin. *From Apples to Applesauce*. Mankato, Minnesota: Capstone Press, 2004.

Wallace, Nancy Elizabeth. *Apples, Apples, Apples*. Tarrytown, New York: Marshall Cavendish, 2004.

Videos

Buell, Bruce. *Apple Farming for Kids*. Victor, NY: Rainbow Communications.

Web Sites

Apples and More
www.urbanext.uiuc.edu/apples/

Kids Health Recipes: Awesome Applesauce
kidshealth.org/kid/recipes/recipes/applesauce.html

U.S. Apple Association Kids' Page
www.usapple.org/consumers/kids/index.cfm

USDA: MyPyramid.gov
www.mypyramid.gov/kids/index.html

About the Author

Dana Meachen Rau is an author, editor, and illustrator. A graduate of Trinity College in Hartford, Connecticut, she has written more than two hundred books for children, including nonfiction, biographies, early readers, and historical fiction. She likes to pick apples with her family near her home in Burlington, Connecticut.

About the Reading Consultant

Nanci R. Vargus, Ed.D., wants all children to enjoy reading. She used to teach first grade. Now she works at the University of Indianapolis. Nanci helps young people become teachers. Homemade applesauce is a family favorite.

Marshall Cavendish Benchmark
99 White Plains Road
Tarrytown, NY 10591-5502
www.marshallcavendish.us

All Internet addresses were correct at the time of printing.

Library of Congress Cataloging-in-Publication Data

Rau, Dana Meachen, 1971–
Applesauce / by Dana Meachen Rau
p. cm. — (Benchmark Rebus : What's Cooking?)
Summary: "Easy to read text with rebuses explores how to make applesauce"—Provided by Publisher.
Includes bibliographical references.
ISBN 978-0-7614-2894-7
1. Cookery (Apples)—Juvenile literature. 2. Applesauce—Juvenile literature. I. Title.
TX813.A6R39 2008
641.6'411—dc22
2007022889

Editor: Christine Florie
Publisher: Michelle Bisson
Art Director: Anahid Hamparian
Series Designer: Virginia Pope

Photo research by Connie Gardner

Rebus images, with the exception of applesauce and tree, provided courtesy of Dorling Kindersley.

Cover photo by Maya Barnes Johansen/The Image Works

The photographs in this book are used with permission and through the courtesy of:
Stephen Mark Needham/Jupiter Images, p. 2 (applesauce); CORBIS: p. 3 (tree); Getty Images: p. 5 DAJ; p. 7 Adie Bush;
Photo Edit: p. 9 Myrleen Ferguson Cate; Jupiter Images: p. 19 Simon Watson; DK Images: p. 11 Dave King;
The Image Works: p. 13 Sven Picker; p. 21 Maya Barnes Johansen; Corbis: p. 15 Senthil Kumar; p. 17 Roy Morsch.

Printed in Malaysia
1 3 5 6 4 2

31901050265844